Arctic Hares

by Rebecca Pettiford

BELLWETHER MEDIA • MINNEAPOLIS, MN

BLASTOFF!
2
READERS

Note to Librarians, Teachers, and Parents:

Blastoff! Readers are carefully developed by literacy experts and combine standards-based content with developmentally appropriate text.

Level 1 provides the most support through repetition of high-frequency words, light text, predictable sentence patterns, and strong visual support.

Level 2 offers early readers a bit more challenge through varied simple sentences, increased text load, and less repetition of high-frequency words.

Level 3 advances early-fluent readers toward fluency through increased text and concept load, less reliance on visuals, longer sentences, and more literary language.

Level 4 builds reading stamina by providing more text per page, increased use of punctuation, greater variation in sentence patterns, and increasingly challenging vocabulary.

Level 5 encourages children to move from "learning to read" to "reading to learn" by providing even more text, varied writing styles, and less familiar topics.

Whichever book is right for your reader, Blastoff! Readers are the perfect books to build confidence and encourage a love of reading that will last a lifetime!

This edition first published in 2019 by Bellwether Media, Inc.

No part of this publication may be reproduced in whole or in part without written permission of the publisher. For information regarding permission, write to Bellwether Media, Inc., Attention: Permissions Department, 6012 Blue Circle Drive, Minnetonka, MN 55343.

Library of Congress Cataloging-in-Publication Data

Names: Pettiford, Rebecca, author.
Title: Arctic Hares / by Rebecca Pettiford.
Description: Minneapolis, MN : Bellwether Media, Inc., 2019. |
  Series: Blastoff! Readers. Animals of the Arctic | Audience: Age 5-8. |
  Audience: K to Grade 3. | Includes bibliographical references and index.
Identifiers: LCCN 2018030986 (print) | LCCN 2018036174 (ebook) |
  ISBN 9781681036601 (ebook) | ISBN 9781626179400 (hardcover : alk. paper)
Subjects: LCSH: Arctic hare--Juvenile literature. | Animals--Arctic regions--Juvenile literature.
Classification: LCC QL737.L32 (ebook) | LCC QL737.L32 P485 2019 (print) | DDC 590.911--dc23
LC record available at https://lccn.loc.gov/2018030986

Editor: Rebecca Sabelko   Designer: Jeffrey Kollock

Printed in the United States of America, North Mankato, MN

Table of Contents

Arctic hares live on Arctic mountains, rocky **plateaus**, and treeless coastlines.

4

Their long, thick fur keeps them warm in this cold **biome**.

Arctic Hare Range

N
W ✦ E
S

range =

Arctic hares have gray
and brown summer fur.
It matches the color of
the land.

Their fur turns white each winter.
It looks like the snow.

black-tipped ears

Arctic hares have black-tipped ears that take in heat from the sun.

Black eyelashes act like sunglasses. The eyelashes guard their eyes from snow **glare**.

eyelashes

Arctic hares are fast! Their powerful back legs help them escape **predators**.

Their large feet keep them
from sinking into the snow.

Arctic hares have thick fur on their paws. It keeps them warm.

Special Adaptations

black-tipped ears

sharp claws

large, fur-covered feet

It also keeps them from slipping on ice and snow.

Power in Numbers

To keep warm, Arctic hares sit on their legs and flatten their ears.

When it is very cold, they group together.

Arctic Hare Stats

Least Concern	Near Threatened	Vulnerable	Endangered	Critically Endangered	Extinct in the Wild	Extinct

conservation status: least concern

life span: 3 to 5 years

Arctic hares sometimes feed in groups, too. If a predator arrives, they **scatter**.

The predator does not
know which hare to chase!

Finding Food

In summer, Arctic hares eat berries, roots, buds, and leaves.

In winter, they eat dwarf willow, mosses, and **lichens**.

Arctic Hare Diet

dwarf willow

lichens

crowberries

Arctic hares have sharp claws that they use to dig for food.

Adaptations like this make the Arctic the perfect home!

Glossary

adaptations—changes an animal undergoes over a long period of time to fit where it lives

biome—a large area with certain plants, animals, and weather; Arctic hares live in the Arctic tundra biome.

glare—a strong, bright light that shines off of something

lichens—plantlike living things that grow on rocks and trees

plateaus—areas of flat, raised land

predators—animals that hunt other animals for food

scatter—to separate and go in different directions

To Learn More

AT THE LIBRARY

Arnosky, Jim. *Frozen Wild: How Animals Survive in the Coldest Places on Earth*. New York, N.Y.: Sterling Children's Books, 2015.

Phillips, Dee. *Snowshoe Hare*. New York, N.Y.: Bearport Publishing, 2015.

Riggs, Kate. *Arctic Tundra*. Mankato, Minn.: Creative Education, 2015.

ON THE WEB

FACTSURFER

Factsurfer.com gives you a safe, fun way to find more information.

1. Go to www.factsurfer.com.

2. Enter "Arctic hares" into the search box.

3. Click the "Surf" button and select your book cover to see a list of related web sites.

Index

The images in this book are reproduced through the courtesy of: Sophia Granchinho, front cover, pp. 18-19; Visual & Written SL/ Alamy, pp. 4-5; Biosphoto/ SuperStock, p. 6; sirtravelalot, pp. 6-7; Paul Loewen, pp. 8, 10, 14-15 (left cutout), 20-21; age fotostock/ SuperStock, pp. 8-9; evgenii mitroshin, pp. 10-11; Ilukee/ Alamy, p. 12; Design Pics Inc/ Alamy, p. 13; All Canada Photos/ Alamy, pp. 13 (bubble), 14-15; Pierre Vernay/ biosphoto, pp. 16-17; Michal Hykel, p. 19 (dwarf willow); Tamara Kulikova, p. 19 (lichen); Lev Komarov, p. 19 (crowberry); Olga Alexandrova, p. 22.